MY FIRST LOOK

AT SEASONS

A BRIDGE READY FOR A WHITE CHRISTMAS

Winter

Jill Kalz

CREATIVE EDUCATION

Published by Creative Education

123 South Broad Street, Mankato, Minnesota 56001

Creative Education is an imprint of The Creative Company

Designed by Rita Marshall

Photographs by Dennis Frates, Getty Images (Wayne R. Bilenduke), George Robbins, Tom

Stack & Associates (Ann Duncan, Jeff Foott, John Gerlach, Thomas Kitchin)

Cover illustration © 1996 Roberto Innocenti

Copyright © 2006 Creative Education

Printed in the United States of America

Library of Congress Cataloging-in-Publication Data

Kalz, Jill. Winter / Jill Kalz.

p. cm. — (My first look at seasons)

ISBN 1-58341-365-0

1. Winter—Juvenile literature. I. Title.

QB637.8.K35 2004   508.2—dc22   2004056164

First edition 9 8 7 6 5 4 3 2 1

WINTER

Short Days, Long Nights

December is here! The air feels colder. Snow may fall. Many people shop for Christmas presents. In the northern half of the world, December 21 is the first day of winter.

Winter is one of Earth's four **seasons**. The other seasons are spring, summer, and fall. Each season lasts about three months. Winter comes between fall and spring.

LEAVES COVERED BY ICE CALLED FROST

Winter days are the shortest and coldest of the year. The sun rises late each morning and sets early each night. On cloudy, cold days, snow may fall.

Snow looks beautiful, but it can be dangerous. A windy snowstorm is called a blizzard. Blowing snow makes it hard for people to see during a blizzard.

In 1953, one part of Alaska
got more than 15 feet (5 m)
of snow in one week.

WINTER STORMS CAN BE VERY WINDY

A FOREST COATED WITH LOTS OF SNOW

Sleeping Plants

Plants need warmth and water to grow. Many plants die in winter. The air is too cold for them. Water usually turns into ice in winter, so plants have nothing to drink.

Not all plants die in winter. Some go to sleep. They make a lot of food in their leaves in summer. They keep the extra food in their **roots**. During winter, this food keeps the sleeping plants alive.

SOME APPLES HANG ON BRANCHES IN WINTER

Grass sleeps through winter. Trees and bushes sleep, too. Their leaves may turn brown or fall off, but the plants are still alive. They will wake up again in spring.

Living in the Cold

Before winter starts, many animals **migrate**. Others get ready to live in the cold. Rabbits grow thick fur. Birds grow more feathers. Mice huddle together to stay warm.

Some insects spend

winter wrapped in cocoons.

Cocoons look like

little sleeping bags.

MANY BIRDS LEAVE THEIR NESTS AND FLY SOUTH

Food can be hard to find in winter, so some animals **hibernate**. They eat a lot of food in fall. Then they find a safe place to rest. Chipmunks, gophers, and turtles hibernate. So do snakes and frogs.

When an animal hibernates, it breathes slower. Its heart beats slower. And its body cools down. Hibernating animals do not move much until spring.

New Year's Day, Valentine's Day,

and St. Patrick's Day

are all winter holidays.

THIS RABBIT'S FUR BECOMES WHITE IN WINTER

A Wonderful Season

Winter has a lot of **holidays**. Hanukkah, Christmas, and Kwanzaa are winter holidays. Each holiday is different in many ways. But each one brings families together.

During these holidays, people may give presents. They may sing songs or decorate trees. They might light candles and go to church.

A house decorated for Christmas

Many people do things outside in winter. Some people go ice skating or skiing. Others go sledding. Some people fish through holes on frozen lakes.

Winter is a wonderful season. Enjoy it! Build a snowman! Put food out for the birds! Sing a holiday song! And then, get ready for spring!

SOME PEOPLE GO ICE FISHING IN WINTER

HANDS-ON: FEED THE BIRDS

Surprise your bird friends with this treat!

WHAT YOU NEED

Plain popcorn

Yarn

A plastic sewing needle

WHAT YOU DO

1. Have a grown-up help you thread the needle.
2. Carefully push the needle through a piece of popcorn. Slide the popcorn toward the end of the yarn. Stop at least six inches (15 cm) from the end.
3. Add more popcorn. Stop at least six inches (15 cm) from the other end.
4. Have a grown-up help you tie the yarn in a tree. Or tie it to a fence or railing. Then watch the birds eat!

A WOODPECKER ENJOYING A TASTY TREAT

INDEX

WORDS TO KNOW

hibernate—go into a very deep sleep for weeks or months

holidays—special days that happen every year

migrate—move from one place to another, usually to find warmth or food

roots—the parts of plants that grow underground

seasons—the four parts of a year: spring, summer, fall, and winter

READ MORE

Bancroft, Henrietta, and Richard G. Van Gelder. *Animals in Winter*. New York: HarperCollins Children's Books, 1997.

Chocolate, Deborah M. Newton. *My First Kwanzaa Book*. New York: Scholastic, 1999.

Kalman, Bobbie. *What Is Hibernation?* New York: Crabtree Publishing Co., 2001.

EXPLORE THE WEB

CLAUS.COM http://www.claus.com

HanuKat http://www.hanukat.com

Kids Domain: Winter Fun http://www.kidsdomain.com/holiday/winter